YEAH YEAH YEAH

YEAH YEAH YEAH

Roddy Lumsden

BLOODAXE BOOKS

ISBN: 1 85224 403 8

First published 1997 by
Bloodaxe Books Ltd,
P.O. Box 1SN,
Newcastle upon Tyne NE99 1SN.

Bloodaxe Books Ltd acknowledges
the financial assistance of Northern Arts.

Cover printing by J. Thomson Colour Printers Ltd, Glasgow.

Printed in Great Britain by
Cromwell Press Ltd, Broughton Gifford, Melksham, Wiltshire.

Acknowledgements

Acknowledgements are due to the editors of the following publications in which some of these poems appeared: *Poetry Introduction 8* (Faber & Faber, 1993), *Dream State: The New Scottish Poets* (Polygon, 1994), *The Gregory Anthology 1991-93* (Sinclair-Stevenson, 1994), and in *Cambridge Journal of Contemporary Criticism, New Writing Scotland, Rebel Inc, The Rialto, Scratch* and *The Wide Skirt*. Some of the poems were published in two pamphlets, *Elsewhere Perhaps Later* (privately printed, 1995) and *new poets series 1* (*ibid* press, 1996), the latter shared with Kate Lowenstein. 'Then' won first prize in the *poetry postcard quarterly* competition 1995.

The author wishes to thank the Society of Authors for an Eric Gregory Award and the Scottish Arts Council for a Writer's Bursary and a Writing Fellowship. Thanks also to my parents for their support and to Andy Jackson for perceptive help in editing.

Contents

I.

COMING

GRANNY: Did you throw a penny in the wishing well?
TODDLER: Yes.
GRANNY: What did you wish for?
TODDLER: To make a big splash.

– overheard at Earlshall Castle, Fife, 1987

Beauty is only one of your faults.

– recommended chat-up line

Then

For the first time, I listen to a lost
and secret recording of us
making love near-on ten years ago.

I recognise your voice, your sounds,
though if I knew no better,
I could be any man in any room.

After, the rising sounds of rising
and of dressing and once
as you step up close to the deck,

perhaps to pick up shoes, you sing
the chorus of *Sunday Morning.*
I call on you to hurry and we leave.

It does not end then; the tape rolls on.
A few late cars which sigh by
might have passed us walking away

triumphant, unaware we've left behind
this mop and mow mechanism
of silence to which we may never return.

Sunday Morning 2.13 a.m.

What did we ever solve, in this hooked-in corner
of the night? All we could pause to hear
were minimals of sound – a wafer shifting
in the floor-draught, the butter-sucking mouse
poised and looming in its minor world.

The city's cowled quiet now, with shadows
where nothing will move save tensions
in the mood of light. I know of you this way –
folded in the brood of your sleep, far from here
in miles and in years – semi-precious, imprecise.

Sweetard

She cried a moment after being born.
Her father has (or had) at least one daughter;
Her mother's old enough to be her mother.

She smiled at Mickey Mouse when she was young
And Coca Cola bubbles starred her tongue.
She buys her clothes in one shop or another.

She earned more ticks than crosses when at school
And had a crush on someone in her teens.
Sometimes she wears a skirt, and sometimes jeans.

She is, but wishes she was, beautiful
And crawls into a bed each night and pulls
Her duvet up and falls into a dream.

She does not know my name. That much is clear.
And beer goes up ten pence a pint a year.

Seat Still Warm

I slide an ill-considered arm
Around the guilty past. No harm,
Should it hiss at a willing caress.

I tip the pyxis, up the dose
And wait for what is comatose
To wake in a moment of weakness.

I see through the placebo now
It leaches on my tongue, and how
The bitterness smacks of finesse.

I ease into the seat still warm
With things on which I won't be drawn,
Or exchange for the brightest of secrets.

St Patrick's Day

the 16th – her

A dream ghost in a naval cap
came calling in the night:
'Your father's lost at sea.' Her father,
a shop manager, three years now
in the Garden of Remembrance,
had taken a dinghy out, odd times,
but always had returned safe,
his hair tossed, cheeks too red.
All day, a slight touch of something;
children in next door's garden,
the radio not quite tuned in.
'Lost, but not at sea,' she said
and turned in with some milk
warmed in a pan on the stove.
The usual sleepy half-promises,
the usual almost perfect silence.

the 16th – him

A day to give up sport, perhaps.
The captain bore down on him
in the changing room: 'Things on
your mind?' Indeed. Find time now,
to change this, all subjects. He could
have gone on to the clubhouse,
a row of gold on the drip-plate,
news of wives-to-be, ex-wives-to-be.
The stereo gone on the blink again;
the haw of the kettle – poor man's music.
No longer willing part of any team,
can't be bothered with this whisky.
The TV brays throughout the evening.
In bed, it seems the rain might just
break through. Get up again, take
the third and hottest shower of the day.

the 17th – I

Two journeys which, in joining,
find their sense. They'd started out.
For her, the Sunday papers – him,
some breakfast, late, consolatory.
It's no one's fault. Though she, perhaps,
or he might have given way. Anyhow,
by the fire station, they crash. A moment
of anger before faces are taken in.
Words and details swapped, they end up
taking lunch at The Hound. Mistaking
the spring's false start for summer,
she walks to the car-park in short sleeves,
head full of two glasses of house red.
He's signed the cheque. It's no one's fault
and no one saw it coming. What's lost
but paintwork? This is a good man's day.

the 17th – II

'That second glass!' she says. He drives
and stops to buy her papers, pays again
and brings the only flowers in the shop:
'To say sorry.' But they both know this
apology's a sham. More than meets the eye.
She contradicts and smiles and tilts
her head back on the rest. Back home,
he puts on coffee: 'Place is such a mess!'
But she is reading, not reading, calls back,
'Make it black,' and softly, under breath,
has placed an "and" between their names
to try the sound. Tomorrow's work, still
hours and hours away, and later he will
watch the way her toes move up against
the cushion, feel her hair's weight on
his lap. The stereo works for once.

the 18th – him

The morning's full of must-be-done.
The mooring place – the bed (found
unmade shamefully the night before) –
creaks under double cargo. She is first
to go. He shaves and leaves the mail
unread, his collar button loose beneath
his tie. The weekly pep talk: 'Teamwork!
Keep the spirits up!' And his are flying.
In his desk diary, by the date, he draws
a four-leaf shamrock and a Star of Hope.
The sharp sun through Venetian blinds,
the day's a blur. 'What's with you today?'
He knows, but keeps it to himself for now.
Cross town, the hammers crash, the dents
are taken out. A brand new headlamp
fixed in place. Car, everything, set anew.

the 18th – her

Back home, she draws her work clothes on,
but calls in sick, falls back to sleep.
At noon, she puts her teacup on the floor,
in camisole and leggings, searches through
old piles of photos, cousins' weddings,
father in his army days. The phone rings
and she lets it ring. At last, she finds
the one; she's five then, feeding swans,
her face a promise. Later on, she takes
a slow walk to The Hound and finds
her car. She laughs. The damage done
is minimal. Thus far. This thought
and that thought cross her mind. At sea.
In the doorway of the pub, a sign says,
'Spend St Patrick's Day at The Hound'.
When no one's looking, she pulls it down.

Coincidence, Mate

I'm absent-mindedly attempting a little algebra –
how they hoik the amount of prawn crackers
on the set meals menu at the Imperial Palace
(at what pace, say; how many wax-paper bags?),
when the synaptic pinball bumps again against
the chances of her name and that word paired
by any hand which I would try and fail to forge.

Bewildered, I determine to claim the kitchen
for Scotland but find the kettle steaming,
flags of underwear drying on a chair-back
and a scrawled message which seems to read,
'Lindbergh, Earhart and Johnson all believed
they were flying solo', which I duly scrunch
and send into the dustbin in a tremendous arc.

I'll make my point – there is no malison involved:
he got there first and never thought to check
behind for me, whose exigence was held up
by the urge to find a perfect route (coincidence,
you'd say: no one is flying solo, no uncharted lands,
but careful how you step), my chance now gone
to write her name and to define her first.

Manners

I'd squirreled them like rations for
emergencies which might yet come:
the protocol of hand on hip,
the solemn rule of thumb
on flesh, quoting the tournure of a breast.

And had there been a thunderstorm,
whisky on ice instead of wine,
some purpose soaking through the hour,
we might have realigned
the courtesy which kept us dry and dressed.

If blame is down to details, if
you're lost, and if thereby it proves
that manners make the man, and not
that fundamental move
which splits the sky, is anybody's guess.

Coming

Outside the cinema, all evening long,
there is a young man waiting on
the girl who isn't coming.

I watch him stand and smoke and weep,
or crouch down, head in hands,
till one last audience files home to sleep.

And only now do I get to thinking
how the tenpenny hole in his trouser-seat, to me,
is the winking light of a buoy at sea

that marks what is hidden
and the way death comes in to land,
perfect and sudden.

364

On the long, last day of my twenties,
I am plugging a quiz machine
in a dark saloon in the Cowgate.

Beside me, a couple are pushing through
that 'for the best' scenario,
tugging each way till the air is static.

She is Australian, weeping, and sports
a navel ring, an anti-symbol,
while he is foppish, hugging, tries too hard.

It is only in the moment of chaos
we realise what the half-moon
is a half of, what our breath is a gulp of.

Later, when they make a film of this,
my character is younger, handsome
and altogether missing from that scene.

Fattening

I tell her that the glistening is goodness,
that the glistening is stars. Reachable.
All that we ever wished for and more besides.

We both know what the glistening is: that it's
the ounce knob of butter I've stirred into
her soup. That I'm treating her like a child.

It's true to say that I want her body back
for my own reasons too. I gave up
philanthropy per se when I stepped off the Ark.

I stand in the open bathroom doorway, fix her
with a stern look as she squats to pee.
Her days of going in alone are over for the time being.

A glass bottle full of mouthwash catches me
on the temple. 'Now we're both martyrs,'
she'll say, admiring the yellow of the bruise.

But I'm doing the right thing, aren't I? Didn't we
make promises once, lying out in long grass
at... where was it? We take turns on the scales,

while through in the next room, on the stereo,
some long ago crowd raises a cheer as,
one by one, they recognise what song this is.

Yeah Yeah Yeah

No matter what you did to her, she said,
There's times, she said, she misses you, your face
Will pucker in her dream, and times the bed's
Too big. Stray hairs will surface in a place
You used to leave your shoes. A certain phrase,
Some old song on the radio, a joke
You had to be there for, she said, some days
It really gets to her; the way you smoked
Or held a cup, or her, and how you woke
Up crying in the night sometimes, the way
She'd stroke and hush you back, and how you broke
Her still. All this she told me yesterday,
Then she rolled over, laughed, began to do
To me what she so rarely did with you.

Common Sense

You had it good for far too long: your wife,
The house, cash rolling in, the foreign trips,
As week by week I loosened and unzipped
And laid my envy bare and longed your life
To stutter: just one slip on ice to leave
A leg in plaster, junkie thieves to clear
Your home of hi-fi, white goods, golfing gear;
Some trauma to allow me to believe
It wasn't personal. And here she sits
Within the year; suggesting I should try
This Gucci suit and picking through the ties
('*He had your build,*' she says). And yes, it fits
A treat. What worth is taste without the touch?
She really doesn't seem to miss you much.

Prayer To Be with Mercurial Women

Let me never have her father
call me, saying how's about
a round of golf? Instead I'll take
the grim, forbidding monster
who inspects me for a crooked
trouser crease. And spare me too
from palmy evenings which sail by
in restaurants, on barstools,
without a storming off or two.
'Darling, you were made for me.'
I pray I'll never hear those words.
I need to feel I'm stealing
love another man would kill for.
When in sleep she curls herself
around me, may she whisper names
that are not mine. I'd prefer
to be the second best she's had.
A curse on mouths which dovetail
as if there'd been a blueprint made:
I'd rather blush and slobber.
And once a month, please let me be
a punchbag. I'll take the blame
for everything: I want to taste
the stinging of a good slap.
I hope I'll find my begging notes
crumpled, torn in half, unread,
and when I phone, I want to hear
an endless sound of ringing.
Help me avoid the kind of girl
who means things when she says them,
unless she's screeching, telling me
exactly what I am. Amen.

Box

On High Riggs, there's a small boy
pushing his companion into
a cardboard box, pressing the lid down.

Of course, it makes me think of
the box I pushed you into
in the early hours of this morning –

the same box I'd just struggled out of,
shrugging and demanding answers.
And of course, it makes me wistful,

so much so that I don't look back
to see them changing places,
parcelling each other, turn by turn.

Turning up my Home Street stairwell,
I glare at my shadow on the wall,
sensing freedom there, and only later

do I realise that for every box I step
out of, there will be another
and another, until the one that fits me.

I.D.T. I.N.D.T.

Honest to God, their love was that thin
you could use it as a needle, seize it
like a nettle or count it on one finger.

Walking on the beach, they appeared
as newly shipwrecked; dancing
was a simultaneous epileptic fit.

Their gifts were mawkish, pink-inked,
destined for the backs of cupboards,
jumble sales, for whoever came next.

Their picnic was no picnic. At the cinema,
the film ran backwards. Their friends
opened a book on how long it would last.

When and if you crept up close to them,
you could just about hear the sound
of *amor* trying to *vincit* crumbs of *omnia*.

Trespass

The sign said PRIVATE PATH and so we veered,
Drawn woken into possibility
Where, fifty yards ahead, it disappeared
In rusty shade below untended trees.
And just around that corner seemed as good
A place as any I might ever find
To hush her and to ask her if she would.
But then I saw him, cowering behind
A fallen oak, his matted, rocking head,
His thorn-stung nakedness. She tugged my hand
And whispered something. Nothing more was said;
We doubled back towards the light. Whose land
It was I couldn't say. But then, who says?
From then, our days were nights, our nights were days.

Wedding Dress

Not enough to stand here thinking,
'Who will wear it?' and press my hand
against the glass, to watch those smudgy
marks dissolve and disappear.

The mannequin, uncompromised
by shadows, cuts its pristine stance.
Across the city, heads and hearts
are filled and emptied. Unconvinced,

I stay and watch, as if the groom
might tap me on the shoulder, guests
spill out from cars. It's not enough
to ask it. Days will disappear,

unsolved, or else will knot themselves
and might not let a fat man through.
This window's clouded by my breath –
I tap the glass and say her name.

Slow Blues

(an epithalamium)

They've been gassing through so many scenes –
intimate, ultimate, out of it –
crowding canvas, a mess of things. Who'd guess

That this might be my wedding song for them?
All claim them doomed, in whispers
or when neither is swanning in the room.

And if there had been time? There might have been
a sunset walk at Arisaig, white beaches –
the sort of tack that blushing, local grooms

with foreign brides aspire to. Slow blues.
For crying over later. Aye, instead,
the single bed they left just hours back.

By any chalk, she's not the first 'I do' in black.
His bellows weren't primed for speeches.
Which crossroads was it where he chose to lose

His soul? Hell knows, but then a Delta bray like his
may later come in handy. Hark at us!
All tut and doubt, we talk in daunted tones about

a Home Office letter which might have arrived.
They're gassing through: the downwind bride
in need of anchor, less in need of altar

and the blue-eyed belter parading his Bianca.
What I wish them's this – not blues at all –
that they wake up this morning to whichever kiss.

On a Promise
(an epithalamium)

And if not caution, then its conduit
Is given to the wind. A giddy ship
Of fools and family, rocking loose (to wit,

There's drink and dancing), witness as you slip
The foolish purchase freedom had become.
Then, clutching at complexity, we strip

The willow, strange brutes turning in a hum
Of shuttles, stripped of any code of dress,
And swirling girls who gracefully succumb

To gallivanting into breathlessness.
And in complexity, accessory
To a loom more excessive than this mess

We mimics weave on, a promissory
Rationale emerges (and not by chance,
There's method in this), a necessary

Arrangement we have conjured from the dance
To celebrate that promises are made
And bargained down, from bittersweet advance

To oath of no retreat, that best schemes laid
To last still can, to scold the cynic's tongue.
No one would claim the tune won't be replayed,

That other hearts won't race, bells hang unrung,
But such shapes aren't fashioned to go through
A repetition. Something is begun.

Some things are made just once, and made for you.

II.

SWANNING

A licence to pity is a privilege many of us have not yet earned. It's not for the likes of us to lick the cuts of the feckless, the inane, the other dissolute. The best we can offer is to keep our eyes down, press the glass to our lips and wish for death to come soon or never.

– CARRICK WILLIS, *The Likes of Us*

Will not your 'truth' always show a disturbing tendency to dance with your 'lies'?

– BRENDAN KENNELLY

Noyade

To start with, the pricey but possible: bottles
of Hennessy XO which we nip down in thimblefuls,
flutes from a twelve year old Krug jeroboam,
a couple of sweet Cuban breezes to loosen the tongue.

A razor of schnapps while the jukebox cranks up,
then the Armalite, tiger-bite, the test-tube traffic light,
the road to Damascus is long, ma cherie, have
another, another, the night is yet young, we must live.

This cider I snitched from the sleeping Medusa,
a sip from the hipflask of Zeus and this wine
from the well at the end of the world and the juice
of the lustberry drizzled in tumblers on spirals of ice.

For our shivers, a fresh mug of maté, a flambé of raki.
To warm us, a mulled mash of apples, salt slammers of tears.
Now the folk of the city are foundered in sleep
we will unwind our fears in this waltz and our turning

will seed a new language, will send off new colours,
will settle a matter of time, hold the floor, hang the walls,
shake the windows and, seeping out into the street,
it will ripple and swell. It will swallow them all.

Bout, S. Clerk St

There's this, and some prior disease.
Whatever's next, I'm eaten.
The stink of additives, doctor's books,
things spotted in the winding of the room,

and shapes of the furniture spelling names
of those long gone or damned.
And I'll tell you what this is – just
the wrong time to be thinking about it.

Somewhere close, they've washed and lined up
row on row of glasses. Empty.
Empty to be filled. Filled to be emptied.
A desperate routine when held up to the light,

dropped and splintered. Don't bother searching
for its medical term or Latin name.
It's thirsty work, yanking out the roots
to leave the new skin blotched and bare.

Swanning

Odd, the things you think on, drinking alone:
the difference between *a* void and *the* void,
the spawn site of the conference fish,
the lyrics to *Green Onions*.

And on the way home, the moon leans over
the sill of night and says, in my own voice,
'Hey, Roddy, live slow, die young.'

Even back home, this Venetian blind
becomes a screen which promises,
Coming Soon, *Liberty with a Mermaid's Tail*
and *Babel*, starring Buster Keaton.

St James Infirmly

I *Terra Firma*

It isn't Christblood in the grail tonight.
They're queuing for the hottest show in town,
The fools. St Martin's summer in St James
Has come too early, perfect climate for
The nourishment of next year's crop of crank
And casual staff. I beach that shoddy ark
I call my butt up on a creaking stool
And chew my hangnails, waiting for the flood.
'Pint, Roddy?' It soaks back, a constant drip
Through marinated timbers, lightly oaked,
Onto the Brylcreem basket of my hair.
The CD jukebox pipes up with *There There
My Dear*, a variation on a theme –
Dear barstaff, pull to pour and push to cream.

II *Bonspiel, vs Eleanor*

For this, I waste a summer afternoon –
What's more, an opportunity to drink
My death a little nearer. Up the rink,
I send a lucky curling-stone that's broomed
By *jalousie de métier*, stops short
Of meaningful alliance. Target missed:
Habitual as getting slowly pissed
With booze and blabbering. A dismal sport.
Dìreach an àbhaist, as the Gaels would say
And, *plus ça change*, same as it ever was,
I'm reeling from effect, without a cause,
And ill-prepared to give the game away.
Faint praise, I know. Enough of silly games.
For now. Meanwhile, I'm drinking at St James.

III *Danse Macabre*

On Princes Street, I catch the eye of Death
Which drops its jaw and scrambles for the list
Of its impending squeezes. Name's not there!
It's horny for me though – I'm just its type.
Down in St James, it sneaks in on my tail
And gets in first when I attempt to pay.
It wants to have its way with me. I guess
I'll crumble after six or seven pints
Of cooking lager, lean to take a kiss
That's silver-cold, that sucks my beery breath
Until I'm cross-eyed from it and Elaine
Suggests an early night might do me good.
'She's right,' Death whispers, looking at the time,
'I've got to have you now. Your place or mine?'

IV *The Game of Eyes*

I catch her eye and catch a hailstone, blind,
Which doubles off the snare-skin of my palm.
I clutch the monumental beer glass, find
A custard mantra – 'Yes, I am, I am.'
Once great aunts flicked my lashes, winked and said
The lassies would sweep easily, knocked dead.
Some potion that, that Chalmers aunties cooked –
All right for them, who to a woman looked
Like Riefenstahl was just around the block
To capture them: a female master race
In fading photographs. And now this face
Which measures mine, on forays to the clock:
Albedo of my skimmed irradiance
Already pasteurised with common sense.

V *To Kate*

Dear Sis, look, haven't seen you in a while
But, sorely unempowered by a spasm
Of any flavour north of rank and file,
I'm bulling with you here now, in a chasm
Of howling, tight St Jamesery. I've been
Sat mumbling on a sum of lesser parts
With folks down in that rat-race bar in Queen
Street (a b-maid's birthday – firewater sports,
Of strictly amateur variety),
Then wandered back to base: an August night
Milk-full with distraction. Unwittingly,
(I'd sought to pay my dues, to be polite)
I stumbled, close to dying, on a seam
Of small percentages, on what they mean.

VI *Carracas*

'I'm in the Oyster Bar, and Roddy's bad:
No one knows how much cooking he has had.
St James infirmly, though – must get him out.
What? Oh, sat at the bar, yapping about
The insect life of Portugal and teaching
Some passing punter how to say their word
For sheep-tick. Honest, Kate, you should have heard
Him earlier, a total shambles, preaching
To the converted...' Sintra: Sofia's mutt's
Soused in a caustic bath to loose the keds,
Near on a thousand, each blood-bloated head
Imploding in the poison. Horrid, but
Spot on. Spouting despite that stopgap meal,
My fingers scarlet, stained with cochineal.

VII *A Brief History of Closing Time*

A bawl: 'Last orders at the bar now please!'
The Little Death, which isn't, after all,
A pilfered, pushed-for orgasm, still comes
Served in a woman's voice, breathless and drained;
A grand finale cried by ringing bells.
Then, those for whom it's all but over now
Scrabble for coats and drift towards the door,
Exchanging numbers, wiping upper lips.
Tomorrows are proclaimed and boons invoked.
A trail of five pence pieces on the floor;
A Marlboro in an ashtray, thumbed near dead,
Has shed a dozen keen spittles of fire
From which you cannot turn your gaze until
You count them down through transience, to nil.

VIII *Objet Trouvé*

The following – a message found inside
A sorry-I-forgot-your-birthday card
Discovered in a doorway, walking home
From yet another late night in St James,
And tossed into a drawer, to be perused
At such a time that I might read the words
Without a primal stirring in the gut,
Without the out of character desire
For torture (taking turns, if possible)...
And in my room, a smell of game gone high,
And in my guzzled fog, I hug myself
And squeeze until I feel sufficient pain
To nullify the sweet song in my head,
And pray (I'll spare you what the message said).

IX *Corrida*

The taxi driver looks up as I pull
The curtains. There's a language that subsides
Like promising young men who thought the bull
Would wait until they aged before their eyes
Were dazzled by the point itself, a tongue
Common enough to disengage the young
And steer them from the ring. Try telling them
That it ends up like this: sickness, mayhem
And soda water – all that you can take –
The red rag soaking into the eye's white
And raging for some sleep as early light
Seeps through the room's red curtains. Crimson lake,
That colour in a childhood paintbox which
I dabbled with and never sensed so rich.

X *Katzenjammer*

And by the time I'm dragged up from the sack
By roadworkers, another shift begins
On Calton Road. I'm paying for my sins:
Blood, sweat and tear-wrung minion on the rack
Of consequence, the mirror placed face down
In case I pass and fail to recognise
The swollen, scowling face, the red-shot eyes,
Or worse, lost my reflection on the town.
Host of a crapulous Olympics this
Morning, I improvise a queasy waltz
With coffee, Solpadeine and liver salts.
I flip the mirror, blow myself a kiss.
My patron saint will pluck me from the fight:
It won't be Christblood in the grail tonight.

Mary Millington

Tequila-numb, slumped shambles that we are
at the counter of the St James Oyster Bar
a quarter hour before the call for time.

So, as requested then, the three fine blondes
who come to mind are Ingrid Bergman first,
then Peggy Lee and Mary Millington.

My friend who's next to comatose awakes,
says, 'Each car has its driver, boys,' to which
I nod and cannot find an argument.

I check the door, expecting Mary, bare
as Botticelli's Venus, roped in, plump
upon the half-shell, nursing a fat and brown

Cuban perfecto loosing ash in drills,
anxious to stand the last and sharpest round
of salty slammers, seeing each one down

with kisses wet as rain on Calton Hill.

Love-Lies-Bleeding

Love-lies-bleeding. Amarant.
Everlasting. Angel's plant.
Love-lies-bleeding. Not for me.
Only blood that I can see
is on the toothbrush. In the pan.
Drip from hangnail. Cut on hand.

Amaranthus. Crimson flares.
Say goodbye to mortal cares.
A sip for death. A swig for joy.
The spitting, swilling, roaring-boy.
Love-lies-bleeding. Love got pissed.
Love got lost like love-in-a-mist.

Amaranthus. Passion flowers.
Passion's minutes pass the hours.
Passion's hours are past and spent.
Love-lies-bleeding. Heaven sent.
Heaven looks and heaven sends
drinker's cramps like diver's bends.

Everlasting. Amarant.
Live forever? No, you can't.
Forever's out then? May as well
keel over now and check out hell.
Love-lies-bleeding. Drooping spike.
Follow down. See what it's like.

Dead men's fingers. Old man's beard.
Hell lives up to all I feared.
Lady's fingers scratch and hack.
Last orders called an hour back.
Grab your jacket. Time to leave.
Amaranthus. Picked by Eve.

Plucked by Adam. Lightly stewed,
mixed with hops and grain and brewed.
Call this pub 'The Tree of Life'.
Pissed-up couple, man and wife.
All night lock-in, all day spree,
love's rich pageant, down 'The Tree'.

Love-lies-bleeding. Love's been mowed.
One for sorrow. Two for the road.
And one more for depravity.
For original sin and gravity.
Amaranthus. Milton's bloom.
Empty cans lie round the room.

Everlasting. On the town.
On the razzle. Get one down.
Live forever? What d'you think?
Forever means forever drink.
Love-lies-bleeding. Love can't buy
the pound sign in the barmaid's eye.

Love-in-idleness, farewell,
for life's a bitch and love is hell.
Love-lies-bleeding. The Accused
stands up in court and pleads for booze.
Love-lies-bleeding. Blood's been spilt.
Amaranthus. Never wilt.

Ecosystem

You shouldn't just walk into this and get away with it,
but the dry eye of the barmaid drew me farther in,
an unstrung hero, thick with yesterday's sweat,
so I try, for her sake, to take a bigger part.
So welcome, and look, another barmaid has dipped out
into history. A jealous boyfriend hanging at the door –
he's part of this too. We talk of him often, most days.
The grist of the mill blows in and out
and never sees the draymen or the cleaners.
If you ask at the bar, they'll show you a list
of what we do when we can't be here.

There's enough time to pencil in the cooks,
their trauma-happy families and private lives:
the real broth we feed on here. I myself
don't say too much, just stand and plug
my quiz machine, rose-proud to be
the paragon that I am in my function,
unshaven, admired for a few simple reasons.
I'm in this for the money. That, and to prove
beyond doubt to myself that I could never love
this girl beside me who, dry as bone
(as if nostalgic for the flesh it held), oh sweeter
than new sun, leans to wipe the screen for me.
She and I both know that our official titles
mismatch us. In-house trivvers shall not dally
with junior management. It's written somewhere.
There's a blockade on us getting too close. Threats
of embraces are vetoed from office and kitchen.

These student barstaff – their college courses
are out there moonlighting on them,
up stepladders, picking out the books
in which none of us are ever mentioned.

Look who's coming in, be at the ready.
Those with pens and notebooks should
keep them nearby at all times while
it's happening. Keep everything dry, drier.

Let me introduce you to the man who
cleans our windows. He also empties
the fruit machine with alarming regularity,
and is on first name terms with all of us.
He'll stand you if he's up. He'll tell you so: words
which sound like water gushing down steps.

The grist of the mill blows in and out
and samples our Traditional Fayre, never seeing
the fetchers and carriers who thrive backstage.
There are many I never meet. Who, for instance,
washes the overalls, who delivered this fine malt?
And the top boys are anyone's guess.
I feel some day I may be asked to fetch
clean schooners from our rivals or to say
a few words on the regimen and design
of the system. Is that you winning again,
they say. I needed it. And she who's got me into this
strides over in her uniform and takes my hand,
at first as if to shake it, but then it seems they've
changed the rules. You are a paragon in your function,
she says and draws me close.

And the nightstaff turn up, heavy with
afternoon freedom, the day's dogma.

Look at all the things we have
around the walls, these animal heads
and mirrors and strange old jars and jugs.
I know they please you because you say
you'll come and see us next time you're in town.
That there's the manager, who's quiet
but has a hand of pleasant iron and
makes sure swimming things are kept aside
from flying things and knows the way of both.
We like him. Sometimes I will spend hours
listening to the stock control, wondering why
bottles are given numbers – this, seven, that, ten.
I wonder about the acrostics of the roster,
or what gravity has to do with beer. And they
will watch my machine as I climb my trails,
answering world capitals, monarch's dates,

chart placings of Elvis (one and two) and by and by
you'll see their faces and understand that we live
so well together. We're here to serve you,
animal public with your many tongues and tastes,
now, what was it you were having?

After Entomology

This getting to know you isn't easy,
like fathoming again the difference
between those insects which come in
at the roadside front of the house,
those which appear from a clear
and verdant stasis round the back,

then those which are, at times, found
struggling against the surface tension
in the toilet bowl at the house's centre:
which are entered as Unclassifiable
in my daybook. After entomology,
my two-leggedness, my lax vanity,

my burdened notion of an in-between:
the dark week when the theatre lies
unvisited or those amassed seconds
of radio dead-time, the notes which
skirl ahead while the piper breathes
or treading water, knowing you'll be saved.

(1966-)

I'm listening to *Spem in Alium*
On a mono 1970s Dansette.
My veins still bear a trace of lithium,
My lap, the ash from umpteen cigarettes.
A *noir*ish little scene – I get the feeling
Some camera is filming me, in slo-mo.
At first I strike the Christ pose; next, I'm peeling
Warhol's banana: Little Prince of PoMo.
While one hand dashes off a storyline,
The other holds a baton and conducts
The score: six hundred voices drowned by mine.
Dear lover, don't believe a word I say
When from beneath my nails, I tease the muck:
The rubber, garlic, soap of history.

How It Begins

You know the way it happens, how
it always is and starts: with steps
behind you or some dropped remark.

I feel it now, though cannot know
its distance from me, just how long
until it has me in a snapping palm.

The way that it begins, you'll hear
'that person', an initial glimpse
of artefact or contract; maybe

days and months will linger, yet
it's in your skin. You won't avert
the next step and will take a hand or take

a letter, sink or rise *then* sink
and that's when it starts up again.
I really need to whet my teeth,

get out tonight, a gut of beer.
It's how it always is. Unsummoned
voices fail to whisper at my ear.

On Home Street

These black crosses are
the first pair of eyes
I've stared into in days.

Just as disappointing are
the paintslaps of hair,
haphazard, at either side.

And the red nose, the grin,
mock me. Back inside,
I try to love this new room.

I hug corners, agree to differ
with the paintwork, run
my fingers through the air.

That boy, mother on one hand,
clown painting in the other,
should have drawn a house.

I want a strip of sky,
a dandelion sun, a chimney
with a pig's-tail of smoke.

Lineage

In some small moment, brother, try for size
the names (all five)
of the Woodburn Terrace Airedales,
each bicycle-cum-flying machine,
the scramming code for Grumpy Green;
at least, if all else fails,
the tremendous few who died.

Next, trace the catabasis of disrepair
of toys kept here
for your small children now:
a blue bear stuffed with cousins' tights,
the rabbit with a taste for heights,
by which we'll measure how
the lineage might fare.

But now, in these linking channels which we run
through sand, digging on
until we reach the water,
despite your kids' indifference,
find asymmetric confluence –
this business of lacking a daughter,
the onus of lacking a son.

Boomerang

A lion will outrun a man – you do not need
to see the photographs – a child who cannot read
or write could tell you that. You cannot say you never
stood beneath a streetlamp late at night, the shiver
spiralling until it reached your feet, the rack
of ages pulling one more inch. So you go back
across the open bible that is Fife, to where
your ageing parents wonder at how poor you are,
to dizzy blessings of the fridge and tumble dryer,
the bath, the bed made up with linen sheets, the fire,
the bliss of sleep at last, though later you will wake
and hear the beast there, seething at the garden gate.

Cardinal

To the north
is a dry dock scuppered by rain.

To the south,
there's a hand sticking out of the mud.

To the east
is the lowest point on a plain.

To the west,
you crack open an egg full of blood.

At the centre, your parents attempt to explain
to each other the chances you had.

State of Head

In a scalp paused from a previous suppleness,
hair grows delinquent from triple crowns,
snaffles unlikely directions. Poor thief of space,
it needs to be tied down. Ears worry no one:
one furring into lack, the other buzzing on.

Each eye has its neighbour in for slammers,
comparing notes on the route to redness.
Eyebrows a feast of skews. A few lashes left
in mourning for siblings fallen in the wars.
Temples ripe for target practice. Cheeks hang

like undiagnosed, galling bunts, sparse-haired,
on the underside of a cow. The squab nose,
a windfall, hybrid fruit. Top lip, a strayed bicep
from years of biting, pursing, twitching, from
the jabber of reluctant kisses. Lower lip dry,

prone to the flutter. Teeth still there mostly,
hanging in, like the black dream of a picador.
The pit of the mouth is a shallows of blood
where fleshknots sprout beneath a flagging surface.
Chins lose count and give up. The inebriate tongue

speaks only once, to confirm its name and address.

Quiet Night In

My first in seven years (illness aside):
I mope about the house; I want to talk
and talk until I say one thing I mean.

I run through fifty States, all thirty-seven
Shakespeare plays, the Beatles' Number Ones,
nicknames and grounds of ninety-two league teams.

So used to having sleep's skin peeled for me,
I can't bite in. An hour before the dawn,
I drink the soft sleep of the sober man,

but in that sleep, the little people take
my fingernails and toenails for their saucers;
my thick hair stuffs a mattress for their queen.

Detox

5 p.m. Mister Halfmast, I kick
my mind toward the blues:
Black Coffee, I'll Get By, whatever.

If you walked in on me, you would
find me flinching, drawing out
the needle of my worst thought.

It's a slack film noir that's lacking
a soundtrack. Go get me one
with a smoky sax, with a good dose

of steel-brushed cymbals. Then,
on the way back, red wine,
two bottles, some Gauloises Blondes.

Sit on the floor and look me over
and tell me I'll be okay and then
get the hell out of here. Like now.

Don't you see that I'm the star of
this scene? Let me finish
this thing I didn't want to start.

Infighting

Take this: for nothing here's chiming, vibrating
and all this vainglory and self-deprecating
just goads at the tender parts, gets irritating.

You'll make no advance advocating monopoly
on any vocabulary; even cacophony
needs the needle to make its point properly.

It's true that you find yourself fey and bewitching,
yet always you feel that the itch that you're scratching's
soothed better by far by bravadoes of bitching.

The off-pat flyting, back-biting and threnody
you render and throw up, at will, won't remedy
the rot of your serenading, lute-laden wannabe.

You can't see a barrier without pushing through it;
it's a poor pearl of pathos you don't disintuit
and you now give a doing when once you'd just do it.

You want my advice? Here it is: try removing
the self from your argument – gluts of self-loving
just pudding the gut of whatever you're proving.

That's it on the chin and I'm sure you can take it,
but that shadow you're boxing is me, so please break it
gently. Best wishes, I hope that you make it.

III.

MISSING

Demands? Just this: that the long not feeling
At home should end. Distance. Unbalance.
No wonder. We've placed so much faith in the air
And the air is so silent now we're so well

And truly in it…

– A.B. JACKSON, from *In Memory of R.D. Laing*

They say simple language is ample for the likes of us.
But the problem with those who call a spade a spade is
this: a shovel gets called a spade. A peat paddle, a Scotch
hand or a hod? All spades. A tortoise, a melon and a
kiss stolen from the wigmaker's daughter? You guessed
it. And only the Lord knows what sideshows of sweetness
and atrocity we will crash past as they drag us screaming
all the way back to Babel.

– CARRICK WILLIS, *The Likes of Us*

The Man Who Played The Voice of God

The TV image, so it seemed to me,
was of a breast, the nipple unaroused
and lying flush, which slowly widened out.

A man who played The Voice of God (he had
the least lines in a cast of nine or ten)
saw something similar, returning home

late after drinks, but wasn't fooled like me
and saw the cloud from Little Boy rise up
through fifty years, though neither of us slept.

The Missionaries

We needed them for all our information
On higher sex: that thing with fishes' mouths
Was clarified with photos; fists and froths
And felching and, at last, elucidation
Of undinism, good old urolagnia.
They spread the news. But most of all they showed
What Scotland had been missing was a code
Of anti-ethics. Lists of neophilias
Were swapped on corners, families were crowned
As admirably deviant, we treasured
Those dipping deepest in the lower pleasures
And did so even after word went round
Of how our missionaries, after work,
Would do it quick and quiet in the dark.

Missing

He'd pointed his toes at the Buddha, had given
the finger to Shakti, and there in a clip
of his thumbnail had witnessed nirvana eclipsed.

In the green room, he whistled; in China, he planted
his chopsticks bolt up in a bowlful of rice,
and he whispered to coals in the dead of the night.

He waltzed under ladders and stroked the black dog
and suffered the shudders while talking in tongues
and snuffed powdered diamonds with beautiful ones.

At home, his bedroom was just as he'd left it:
Meccano and Lego, toy cars in a box.
In the drawers there were neat piles of T-shirts and socks.

In the kitchen, a chair and a plate were left ready,
his mother in tears as she stood at the sink
and his name and his face on the carton of milk.

Pegasus

A little think about what's lying drowned
And naked at the bottom of the well:
A hoovered, blootered, bleezing specimen
Who'd got the goss on all the heavy salts
And lesser vitamins, who came to stay
And hinted she could improvise a cake
From nothing much and wore the sort of kit
With plenty hooks and eyes (all later burned),
Who turned too many heads – the other girls
Got nippy and the guys were dropping jaws.
She couldn't take her medicine, passed out
Between two juicers slumped on the settee.
One boy played wing hand shadows on her throat.
I'm pretty sure, thank Christ, it wasn't me.

Hebe

One time, we passed in darkness, you and I,
in a corridor of strangers chewing leaves;
wild beauties, one of whom you recollect
was snuffed inside the month, bound, gagged and drowned
by her own mother.
                              Our own incident
we now interpret somewhat differently.
I reached out to a small light in your eye,
to rub it out. Instead, you say I stole
your drink and spoke a harsh word in your ear
which stayed with you until moments ago.

Noah

Think of him balding, burnt with mine-run drink
with sons chewing the bitter stick all day
who bicker through their endless games of *Risk*
and daughters-in-law combing Oxford St
for each last piece of costume jewellery.

Bereft, arthritic, conjured for too long –
before him, on a table, feathers fall
from where, within his buckram fist, he holds
a small, grey bird he tries but can't let fly
which sputters, takes a full half hour to die.

Hiatus

In this unchosen moment, I shake the lion
by its gristly paw. It's worth his while
to surrender now. He knows that I can kick

his shit-streaked arse halfway to Jericho
and back. Out of the strong? Give me
a break. I haven't got the time right now

for sweet-toothed dribblers waiting around
for bees to swarm. There's a blessed sparkle
in my perfect eye. I've a few new hatchets to bury

in a few old heads. I sit down centre pitch,
suck oranges and regulate my breath.
The second half's not ready for me yet.

Don't judge me by this break in my affairs.
I'll soon burn down your corn. No sweat.
Two shakes. But someday I will yearn to have

a lap to sleep on. My lying tongue will dry
inside my mouth and, hot air nipping at
my scalp, they'll lead me chained out to the pillars.

Mid-life Crises

I *Early Exodus*

'Because I drew him out of the water,'
You hear her say, then name you. Morning rain
Spikes at the ark among the flags, in which
You lie God-rested. Last night you were safe
Among your own, and even strangers cursed
The tabloids calling you a last year's man:
A monicker which you could not equate
With what you saw in double vision (curves
Hampered in silken black). You've woken late
Beneath the blanket laid by putative sons,
Who couldn't know the genesis: her kiss
Which vined you, sent you winding homeward, full
Of bare intention – knowing only this:
These dark shallows from which you may be pulled.

II *Revelation*

Fevered beneath a sheet, constructing lies
(Just like that small, brown bird below a leaf
In boyhood picture prayers proffered to sleep),
You wear the multiple injuries of life
You hauled on like a Sunday Sloppy Joe,
No longer fashion-conscious, though aware
That over Bruntsfield Links, just a stone's throw,
Your childhood sweetheart's supine and laid bare,
A virgin still. You're halfway there by now,
Funking, but anxious to repeat the vow
To have and hold, then, bolder, you stampede
The threshold solo (she has left the keys
Beneath the mat). She gravitates with need.
You lift your veil. She screams at what she sees.

III *Late Lamentations*

Crossing the Tyne (the kraken lies in wait,
A first rate monster in a corridor
Of salt), she reads *Jane Eyre* but quotes instead
Some half-remembered Hardy, incomplete
And incomplete since you are far from her
And farring fast, about to polish off
Your second blonde today, who clamps four limbs
Around you as you come. You hope this is
Your last and only arrogant deceit,
A thin expulsion dousing what caprice
Had brought alive. In years to come, you'll cop
That sex is for the under twenty-fives
And rightly so. But then, other men's wives
Are so... you're getting maudlin now. Shut up.

IV *Apocrypha*

The willow in the schoolyard (blazoning
Its plaque, the names of those, one child each year,
Who never saw the next), sunk by a man
Now long retired, of your father's vintage,
Tilts in the dream from which you start awake.
A little, lost voice, high, threnetic, lilts
A lullaby, 'This day won't come again.'
Outside? Inside? The diagnoses made –
Male menopause and paroniria
Explained – are hardly satisfactory.
From which crowd should you appear to appear?
Which hidden bonds might surface once you've gone?
Then, drifting back, you wish to dream them here,
Your age, alive: those innocents passed on.

August (and Nothing After)

As I sit on the bus down the curve of The Mound,
I catch the chat of the couple in front:
'I hear that Roddy Lumsden doesn't believe
in the soul,' she says, and shakes her head.
'Worse than that,' says he, 'they say he won't
even entertain the concept of the soul.
Is that no awfy?' I smile my wicked smile.
Then, full of grace, we crosscut Princes Street
where buskers ply their breeze and bile
and lovers cheek each other in the heat.
An old man's coughing by the flower stand.
Two girls drop into Milne's Bar for a beer.
Our flag is flying in a hundred lands.
'The punishment has got to fit the crime.'
And rising up from Easter Road, a cheer
as Hibs go three down just before half-time.

Rogation

I

How might I make sure to avoid
girls called Alison at all costs?

Same goes for any woman whose name
is splendoured in the torch

of a torch song, second-hand:
Joannas, Saras, Carolines.

At any one time, a dozen red-eyed men
somewhere, gulping back the lyrics:

'Forgive me my unworthiness',
'My aim is true.'

II

And how do I come to one like her
whose name seems that

of a masque, a rogation flower
or a next-month's craze,

whose name crosses the floor
in the steps of an implausible dance?

Oh for the dry, dependable glide
of a Morag, Moira, Shona,

now a drink comes down the bar
with my name on it.

Fallen

Now the last dregs of the crew have gone,
at the back end of the wood, I stumble on
the crates of apples rotting,

where what will soon be spooling on the screen
as apple yellow, apple red and green
lie browning and forgotten.

They seem the perfect gift to give the man
who has it all. While, cooking in the can,
his motion picture, *Eden*,

awaits certificate, I must begin
to count what he has left, each one a sin
unpicked and unbitten.

The World's End

Supposing you were wrong and I was right,
I was lying through there thinking
of a place where we and the land must part,

of where a child swings on a wire fence
watching, and where might be found
a paperback whodunnit, blown brown,

where a river stalls and seeps into the grass,
where all the footprints lead one way
and no one, on a late shift, stamps your pass,

where a clisp of light in the willow-herb
is what was dropped from the swag
in the chase, or a shred of a Sixties hothouse;

a place some call a border, some an edge,
as if the many missing or a saviour
will rise in welcome when we step over.

Letter to a Former Pupil

My Dear Clotilde,
                   I'm sure you'd love to see
your Alma Mater spoiled with sun today.
I'm sitting in this room you know so well.
A pair of jays are building in the eaves,
the bulbs are sprouting. Summer can't be far.
I'm well. As to your questions, might I please
address them backwards, so to say. It's just,
the one on garlic can be answered with
a simple yes! Though man to man, it may
well differ. Secondly, as to the war
of 1930, I was never there,
although, as you correctly recollect,
I tended to the sick at Almadine,
but Almadine was 1924.
I cannot help you then. Apologies
for that! But if you really must know more,
you could do worse than write to Martin Beck,
or telephone – he does remember you,
I checked with him this morning. Send your best
to Dolly when you see her. Strange to think
of both of you – just girls so recently,
blank pages onto which I wrote a few
short words – successful, married in the West,
and both to Flanner men! Ah well, I must
attempt this third and hardest question you
have posed and try to make the evening post.
It's not an easy one, but here we go.
As far as I'm sure, God does not exist.
For if he did, he'd shout and shake his fist
and speak our names. In short, he'd let us know!
He'd show himself. But God's a thing of taste,
like snuff, Italian wine, kid leather boots.
I thought I saw Him once, among the leaves
of apple trees in my grandfather's yard,
when I was five or six, my head too full
of proud Creation puff from Sunday school.
And there was God! The scowl, the straggle-beard –
some scrumping tramp after my Grampa's fruit!

Indeed, I'm sure that's all God ever was
and Ever More Will Be! And then there's Christ,
The Cuckoo. No, no, no – enough of this,
I sound like some impassioned atheist.
God does exist my dear, he does. It's just
I don't believe in him! (I've stolen that
from Santayana, don't tell anyone.)
God walks among us. Keep your eyes well peeled.
And if he chooses you, you must submit.
Don't feed him too much garlic though, the smell
would conquer continents! I'm making fun
of your naïveté, my dear Clotilde.
That isn't fair. I'll hope to see you soon.
I'm sure you're just as pretty as the day
you left so quickly.

                          Best regards,
                          AK

Quoad Sacra

It begins with the screen stone-green:
you wouldn't know the set was on.
The voice-over begins (a third-choice actor,
woefully miscast, who picks, uninitiated,
through a stormfield of text).
                              The hand-held
pans a parish which taught itself, a steeple
like a big top's king-pole drawing in
the quotidian, the part and parcel. Geese
take to circles, foregoing urge for urge.
There are no jitters, you'll see what you see.
Don't expect a militiaman's spread hand
to cut this short.
                  The first, true sighting
is of children who, leaping, do not seem to land.
Following the camera through a door,
you hear a snapping shut of books, sighs.
'We are not sure if we are wanted.' This
is the last spoken line. The whole thing
has taken so little of your time.
                              And when
the credits roll up through dark, you remark
that one man seems primarily responsible.

Lines to a Missionary

On some dark night, consider this; beware –
your name may be on a menu somewhere.

A little blood will court the nearing barks
of jackals, or an egg-eyed shark

will snoot you in the blackness, homing in
on fine legs, bare and bicycling.

And no one is exempt – these things occur
like so, no matter who you are,

and nothing in the daybooks of the saints,
in *Life and Work* or common sense

will save you from a beast, thought long extinct,
which thinks your throat fit place to sink

its teeth. If chased by hungry crocodiles,
run zigzag, sure, but reconcile

yourself to your position in the chain;
you may escape, but then again

we'll think no less of you for being killed.
The Christian soul is quite inedible

and better ones than you have turned in awe
to tentacle, to lion's claw.

Of the Fittest

One by one (this time round), you'll be led
Into a matriarchal parlour, stumped
Against the anaglypta – stocking shod.
A pedigree of pencilled strokes shows how
Our stalwart bull-calf drew unto his height.
A buxom, hired speakerine calls out
The yea or nay. Screw shibboleths. We need
Those who can say 'I'm six foot one, at least.'

For women, cleavage (hot or cold)'s a must
(Forget it if your bust is strapped with wire).
An upturned-saucepan belly should resound
When gently slapped, the womb elastic, prone.
The toes should splay when pressed into wet sand,
The hands display the nature of the self.
No silkies please, no sulking Jenny Wrens.
Rude health and wet will burke fever and fire.

Read this and weep, boys – size does matter here.
Your pre-plateau tumescence will be clamped
Against this gauge our master joiner built,
From eye to hilt. You'll claim that extra inch,
If Marilyn... that wench is six below.
Cough for us, sir. Your sperm count multiplied
By times-a-night: that's how you will be ranked.
Gird up your pecs. Nice smile! Now off you go.

We have our theory ready planned and typed
In case some weakling boffin, feeling grand,
Should dare to snipe. We treasure sinew, brawn
And Heraclean tendencies. Alive
And Well and Breeding In... that's our paean.
Our twenty year experiment with moths
(Let's name-check Mendel, Galton) has brought on
A plethora of plaudits. We'll survive.

Yet one man's meat... we know, there will be loss,
But never without merit. Face the facts:
The meek are AWOL. Someone must inherit.
A wayside thick with stragglers short of breath
Won't lead to Easy Street, nor can the blind
Lead us across. You look a little sick –
Relax. We don't envisage life or death
Scenarios. But line up now. It's time.

IV.

VANISHING

What's your favourite sandwich?

I have a couple: a toasted baguette with peanut butter
and apricot jam with really cold white wine. *Mmmm.*
Philadelphia steak sandwich is really good. Oh, and a
really good Italian sausage sandwich. But then you can't
beat toasted Swiss and tomato with a little mustard on.
Ooooooh, or Black Forest ham with German black bread.
Oh my God, and coleslaw and Swiss cheese with Russian
dressing.

— KEANU REEVES, *Empire* magazine

As his [*David Hockney's*] interest in photography grew,
he discovered that the splash he'd painted in 'A Bigger
Splash' was not technically correct. But he came to value
'what the eye saw' above what the camera proved true. I
see this as a paradigm of all the modern arts as we app-
roach the millenium: simultaneously, a redemption of
the figurative and a justification of abstraction, and at
the heart of it, simple human arrogance.

— IRENE LACARRA, *Art 1999*

Mercy

And so, on my return, the terrapins,
Two upturned ashtrays farced with viscera,
Are scrabbling at the bathtub's side, par-boiled
And livid, haggling with mortality –
You having gamely carried out your chore,
Though muddling the hot tap and the cold.

Some skin flakes off. We wait a week before
The first succumbs, breaks water belly-up.
Next morning, you are sent to check the tank.
The second peels and pines, pricks you with guilt.
I scour the owner's manual for hints
On mercy killing methods, come up blank.

This calls for some imagination, since,
Too big to flush away, too still alive
For burial, tradition lets us down.
I scoop it out and drop it in a sack,
While you slip out to start the car, and soon
We're driving slowly to the edge of town.

We circle, find a quiet spot – the moon
A single, silent witness to the deed.
It flails, a wriggling terror in my lap.
I settle it shell-up beneath a tyre;
You deftly hold a balance on the clutch,
Accelerate. I listen for the snap.

At first, it won't appear to matter much;
We'll dine out on the story more than once.
The new pair looks much like the tragic one
And, when you tape those labels, Life and Death,
Onto the bath-taps, how we'll stand and laugh,
Though something sharp will snag us, later on.

Before the Interview

Some gifts received were never truly given:
Dark crumbs pressed in the pages of a book;
A red scarf, briskless, languid on a hook;
This thin tea handed to you at eleven
Before the interview. Days waste away,
Ingredients are sieved into a mush
That's quite unpalatable. What was fresh
Is furred. One secretary withers grey,
Dazed in the headlights of a VDU.
The other wastes her lunch-break faxing Heaven,
While through in Personnel, some littlewig
Is warming to the guy who'll get the gig
Before they get around to seeing you.
At least, that's the impression you are given.

Life Class

I never saw her face, for I looked down
The moment she was led into the room
And introduced. At that point, I assume
She wasn't naked, wore some sort of gown
For decency. Perhaps she tied her hair back,
Kicked off her shoes (they say that women tend
To do that stuff) and, stepping to the stand,
Slipped off the robe and threw it on a chair-back,
Then took her place. The others in the circle
Began to draw; I heard the snap of charcoal
Sticks on sugar-paper. They say that maps
Are made by men like me, who never laid
My eyes upon real land, real life, who made
A perfect sketch of my imperfect lap.

Beach Ceilidh

(Pictou, Nova Scotia)

Starters it gets you, everything ploughing –
the music – bugger nuance. Later,
refrains may please or pinch you,
performances are chalked against,
you begin to see a difference between
the fiddler with the quiet eye
and the one with the hop-foot.

From there, it steepens or webs out:
a chorus of unwanted effects.
You cry out for someone to rein in the slack.
Warning notes sound from wet block,
bluff and cove, at any island house
or bonfire site; look for the cloy
of sawgrass smoke, the spoor of cans.

When a new beat won't let up, some buff
claims fado, though you reckon rembetiko.
How much of Europe is here tonight,
immigrant, impetuous? And you, and you.

ITMA

Honeymooning couples blithely hanging out
the DO NOT DISTURB or a Cockney shout

of 'Taxi!' Stewed prunes. All worth a giggle
to them then. The belly dancer's wiggle

of plenty, tawny flesh in a sheik's harem.
A gust up a lady's skirt? They'd scream.

The Great War past, that man about to come:
I suppose we must forgive them.

Poor Noel Coward, sainted for his tat:
today we'd hang him high (if that

were not pernicious). Bones through noses,
and flower fairies teasing in the roses,

next to nothing on, a sort of kiddie porn
for aesthetes. The past is thick with corn

we wouldn't touch, we who have premature
nostalgia, a predilection for the pure

emphatics of the recent: a Seventies rich
with pre-modern, post-evolution kitsch

and spells with fever. Easy to get smitten.
The past rolls over, begs to be rewritten.

Stay calm. We've seen the future and its name
is more or less more of the same.

See, there's Strummer kicking in his amp
and, outside, Formby leaning on a lamp.

Podkopayeva

To pitch the mind in search of higher things,
To prove and polish what is precious seems
To be her aim. The bars from which she swings
Up into flight are burdens and the beam,
A wire on which she walks through time and space.
The floor she tumbles over is a map
Of war-scorched countries tempered by her grace.
Her box-vault has me whispering *Escape!*
For what she offers us is that precision
We wish for in our awkwardness. At last,
We make some sense of geometry again.
And as the markers come to their decision,
We'll rise like Lilia, hearts beating fast,
And judge ourselves against her perfect ten.

Anti-Chaos Eikons

A rare and perfect calm –
the Mary Celeste found bobbing,
the meal prepared and served
and already the terrible weeping
of women a voyage ahead.

*

Like the small boy standing behind
a television interviewee:
feeling I can wave to the world
but requiring your presence
to bring it off.

*

On the lip of the Meadows,
the day after our storm,
a crow's nest lies fallen
whole, in a startled crackle.

*

You count the steps
out and down from the dream
anticipating the usual amount
but stop short.
Unknown to you, there has been
an explosion;
this is what woke you.

*

The papers say the neighbours say
he kept himself to himself.
What they mean is, he couldn't
keep himself to himself
until that last stillness caught him.

*

Auguste and pierrot: clowns
represent drunkenness and death,
our two pure forms of peace.
So why the chaos, the rouse of water,
the horrid axe of laughter?

                    *

On Bruntsfield Links, the lightning hangs
a sky, an arcing boomerang, a man,
in negative. He catches, throws again.

                    *

You stand at the window
expecting a small, flying thing
but you are blocked
by history, by catastrophe,
by the day's classical posture.
What will eventually come
is not small, not flying
nor any one thing.

                    *

My way of outthinking the wolf chaos:
'I'll huff and I'll puff and I'll
blow your house down!' it says.
'Yes, go on, a fine ruin it will make.'

                    *

Across its web, the spider, tacking,
finds a tiny fairy squealing,
four limbs flailing, pin-teeth clicking
or did you never get that feeling?

Fin

The evidence was minimal: no stains,
no trail of blood, just three satsuma skins,
one dressing-gown, in turquoise towelling,

thrown casually on the sofa arm,
and screwed up in the pocket, one page torn
from a diary – in small, neat script, the following:

8.30 – jog with Fanny Blankers-Koen.
9.45 – play chess with Capablanca.
10.30 – dancing lesson, Fred Astaire.

12 noon – deliver theorem to Fermi.
12.45 – send fax to Mao Tse Tung.
1.30 – sit for Lucian ...and so on.

Sergeant MacGrillen chewed his pencil stub
and turned to me, 'That thing through in the tub?
It might just be the body of the century.

Might take some time to suss what happened here.'
I shrugged and settled in an easy chair
and lit the last smoke in my pack of twenty.

The Boy

The old men at the gate were whispering
about what colour ink Drew Meldrum's will
was written in, when instinct drew me near.
My mother ushered me towards the door,
repeated what we'd heard and sent me off.

This was in the days when words were currency –
and good ones kept a man in drink for weeks.
My dad would eke out versions of each tale,
a yarn, a shanty, even epic verse
if connoisseurs were lurking in the midst.

I found him in the snug at Guddler Bob's,
his custom tankard raised above his brow,
two just-off-duty barmaids, eyes a-pop
at what I'd heard so many times that week,
I'd cribbed a fledgling version for myself.

He shushed and introduced me as The Boy
and filled his empty nip glass up with beer
and pushed it at me. Being just thirteen,
I sat there sheepish, giving them the eye,
though neither had a second glance for me.

Not yet. But that's how stories often start –
not with a war or witch or blazing tower
but with The Boy sat quiet by a fire
raked down to embers, tempering the powers
that might sustain him on the darkened road.

I listened to each word my father said.
My pulse popped with a courage in my veins:
I knew at last that I could better him
and laden with this knowledge, out I strode
like Hansel with his pocketful of crumbs.

The Governor's Dog

I wouldn't say I'm not the man they need
but I am neither dangerous nor sly.
I thread my tongue through my remaining teeth
and try to talk their language. By and by,
they'll pull me through the streets into the court.
I dreamed of it last night: they had me tied
with yellow ropes. When I awoke, I thought
I heard a young girl's serenade outside.

It's said, next cell to mine, they keep a man
who loved the mayor's wife, and she loved him.
He knocks at times. I answer if I can
by drumming my good foot against the rim
of the bedcage. Yesterday, the thin guard
brought me in the governor's dog to take
a walk. I took the leash. Down through the yard
and through the trees, there is a shallow lake

where geese are reared. I asked the guard how long
and how far I should go. He stared at me,
he shrugged and left. I eyed the beast, a strong
broad-bellied mongrel. Far as I could see,
this was the test. What do they have me for?
They cannot know the thing I've really done.
My tracks are covered. Now the governor
wants me to walk his dog, it has begun.

You see, I know they'll watch how far I go.
Today, perhaps, the lake. I might look down,
catch my reflection shifting in the slow
drift of the water. Nearby, from the town,
a sound of bells. It may work out that way,
but something in my head is whispering.
I shuffle round, still limping. At midday,
they'll open up my door. They'll push him in.

Roísín's Wolves

You lost a pale cheek in their pelts – dark-mouthed, imaginary wolves
you kept about for company while working round the elements
of difference a child must learn to isolate and steer around:
that business of the stalagmites and stalactites; the vagaries
of viaduct and aqueduct; the fickle stings of wasps and bees.
Toughest of all, perhaps, you found gradations of that numb word 'love'
we use too easily and keep dividing and dividing as
is in our brittle way of things.
                            In turn, those wolves will rouse from sleep
you left them to and one will paw the air for you, a hank of sleek
become at last the seeking beast you sensed yet did not understand,
which whines the night, intuiting the loops of truth you must yourself
untie, untie.
            So let them go, the others, find the difference
in reason, sorrow, moonrise, stealth. You must now keep the best of all:
the wolf which knows it best to kill the shepherd first and not the sheep.

The Ultimate Curve

Not even Raphael could draw that scene
(Though sources hint he tried it more than once)
Where Euclid stooped to pull from where it hid
A grandiose parabola. And then
There's Giotto who, it's said, would reach to pluck
A perfect, hand-drawn circle from midair.
That's kids' stuff though. The duodenal dip,
Duomo or the dromedary's back:
No joy. An egg comes close but offers up
Such meagre pleasure. Easy on the eye
Is not what I've in mind – spectacular
And ready-made – which I resolve to file
Beside two other mysteries of life:
Houdini's death, the name of Jack Sprat's wife.

Vanishing

Inside the box, her heels escape the air.
He hears the hollow silence, turns to where
The blades are catching all eyes in the hush.
His click of fingers touches off a rush
Of cymbals. Now he holds the first blade taut
And steers its whetted edge toward the slot.
She slips out of her costume, checks her face
As he reveals the white dove in her place.
She lingers till the last of the applause,
Collects her things, while back on stage he saws
Himself in half with worry, grins with fear.
The sea of faces knows she'll reappear
Amongst them soon. She slams a backstage door.
Her high heels echo in the corridor.

The Answers

'A / B / LOTS OF THINGS'
*(graffito chalked on the pavement
below my bedroom window)*

to talk a good man up into his noose
to watch him swing and cut him loose

to kick down or cross the hurdles of desire
to interrogate the fire

to brink at it, to undiscover thirst
to get there first

to make the soul enter the iron
to play La Cucaracha on my siren

to ache well, walk upon the seven seas
to take my pride to the disease

to walk face up in the limbic storm
to slough my norm

to paint the town with a brushful of blood
to be the millionth customer of love
to have to have

to widen and to wizen
to listen, listen, listen

to be halfway healed and be hunted
to get just what I always wanted

to have you ever in my sights
yes you, to find my name in lights
to get these answers right

to say hello to everyone who knows me
to make the living this world owes me

to rub my salt right in
to win and win

to get down in two, to last
to step aside and let the bullet past

to see the light to be seen in, to rise
to write the rules of compromise

to bust the sacerdotal
to come hither and be total

to be kind to be cruel to my sisters and brothers
to be self-effacing on behalf of others

to hear behind me the soundtrack lurch
to reheat the cabbage, carry a torch

to never accept the nearest offer
to blithely suffer
to beg to differ

to gaze out from the manes of Pegasus
to diagnose the morbus scotticus

to be fair and to be mistletoe
to be necessarily so

to empty the void, to solve the case
of do or die, to spite my face

to borrow the stars from the dark and to keep one
to be a deep one

to see just how much I can take
to guess the weight of the angel cake
to lie back and fake

to dangle my feet in the sky
to say when and know why

to strut my stuff, to repent at leisure
to struggle for pleasure

to unexplain, to whip the core
from the apple, to make the high score

to find the exit in the theatre of passion
to come back into fashion

to look down proud into the cot
to damn well want what I haven't got

to be a proper thorn in the eye
to go forth and multiply
to love, to die.

NOTES

August (and Nothing After) owes a debt to the poem 'Where Souls Go' by August Kleinzahler.

Hiatus borrows heavily from the Samson story.

I.D.T. I.N.D.T. found carved on school desks next to e.g. AB L(*oves*) CD, standing for 'if destroyed true, if not destroyed true'.

ITMA was a 1940s radio comedy series (it stood for *It's That Man Again*).

Lines to a Missionary: *Life and Work* is a Church of Scotland magazine.

Love-lies-bleeding: the lore surrounding the amaranthus is described in Brewer.

Mid-life Crises: *Early Exodus* starts with a quotation from Exodus 2.10 (the naming of Moses), and lifts from that story and Genesis 9 (Noah's drunkenness). Paroniria is a sleeping condition where the sufferer has constant morbid dreams.

Podkopayeva: Ukrainian Lilia Podkopayeva won Olympic gymnastics gold in 1996.

Quoad Sacra: a former type of Scottish parish under purely ecclesiastical jurisdiction.

ST JAMES INFIRMLY

St James Infirmly: after the blues standard 'St James Infirmary'.

St James Oyster Bar: a pub on Calton Road, Edinburgh.

St Martin's summer: a warm spell in autumn.

There, There My Dear: a song by Dexy's Midnight Runners.

push to pour, pull to cream: directions on the back of beer dispensers.

bonspiel: a curling match.

jalousie de métier: envy of the skills of someone with the same profession as you.

direach an àbhaist: Gaelic for 'same as usual'.

Chalmers: my mother's mother's family, with eleven sisters.

Riefenstahl: the German propagandist film director who filmed the 1936 Olympics, etc.

albedo: a measure of light reflection between heavenly bodies.

carracas: Portuguese word for sheep-ticks or *keds*.

Sintra: a famously scenic town near Lisbon.

Sofia: a Portuguese friend who told me the dog story / drinking allegory in Carracas.